DIVORCE

BY

CHARLES WILLIAMS

the apocryphile press
BERKELEY, CA
www.apocryphile.org

apocryphile press
BERKELEY, CA

Apocryphile Press
1700 Shattuck Ave #81
Berkeley, CA 94709
www.apocryphile.org

First published by Oxford University Press, 1920.
First Apocryphile edition, 2007.

For sale in the USA only. Sales prohibited in the UK.
Printed in the United States of America.

ISBN 1-933993-34-0

TO MY FATHER
AND MY OTHER TEACHERS

Certain of these poems have appeared in the *New Witness*, and two in *A Miscellany of Contemporary Poetry, 1919*.

CONTENTS

Contents

Divorce

(To My Father)

WHEN Love, born first of thought and will,
Ponders what dooms it shall fulfil,
  And knows itself and names,
Sole son of man to meet and dare
All lusts couched in the body's lair
  Till he their fury tames :

From whom his duty shall he learn,
To whom for admonition turn,
  That his young heart may know
What infinite fatality
Life shall wreak on him, nor shall he
  Refuse to undergo?

Whom but such souls as, torn with pain,
Have proved all things and proved them vain
  And have no joy thereof,
Yet lifting their pale heads august
Declare the frame of things is just,
  Nor shall the balance move?

Each to his teachers,—nor of mine,
Though long and lofty be the line,
  Shall any, sir, be set
More high in this poor heart than you
Who taught me all the good I knew
  Ere Love and I were met :

Divorce

Great good and small,—the terms of fate,
The nature of the gods, the strait
   Path of the climbing mind,
The freedom of the commonwealth,
The laws of soul's and body's health,
   The commerce of mankind.

The charges launched on Christendom
You showed me, ere the years had come
   When I endured the strain,
Yet warned me, unfair tales to balk,
What slanders still the pious talk
   Of Voltaire and Tom Paine.

What early verse of mine you chid,
Rebuked the use of *doth* and *did*,
   Measuring the rhythm's beat;
Or read with me how Caesar passed,
On the March Ides, to hold his last
   Senate at Pompey's feet!

What words of grace, not understood
Until the years had proved them good,
   Your wisdom set in me,—
Until the asps of blindness lay
Upon your brows and sucked away
   Joy, sweetness, memory.

Now all the pages of the wise,
Whereon for happiness your eyes
   Were wisely apt to pore,
Upon another's mouth depend,
And friend by step is known from friend,
   And faces seen no more.

Divorce

Now, now the work all men must do
Is mightily begun in you ;
  And the sure-cutting days
Leave you, disfurnished, dispossessed
Of earth, to seek your spirit's rest
  Beyond our mortal ways.

Now, now in you the great divorce
Begins, whose everlasting source
  Sprang up before the sun,
Whose chill dividing waters roll
'Twixt flesh and spirit, mind and soul,—
  Than death more deeply run :

Divorce, sole healer of divorce ;
For our deep sickness of remorse
  Sole draught medicinal,
Which Grief from bitter herbage brews
Where Babylonish waters ooze
  O'er Mansoul's shattered wall ;

Divorce, who cries all mortal banns ;
Chief foreman of the artisans
  Who quarry from Time's pit
New stuff for souls, hewn stone on stone ;
Piercer of hearts, by whom is shown
  Death in death implicit ;

Divorce, itself for God and Lord
By the profounder creeds adored :
  Who in eternity,
A bright proceeding ardour, parts
The filial and paternal hearts,
  And knits the riven Three.

Divorce

O if in holier hours I meet
Your happier head in Sarras' street,
   When our blind years are done,
What song remains shall run to pay
Its duty, sir, from me that day,
   Your pupil and your son.

In Time of War

I. PRAISE OF DEATH

On this side sit the old men
   Amid their policies,
On that side play the children
   With young unknowing eyes;
Betwixt, encompassed with our fears,
Ascend the dedicated years.

The heads of all male children
   Were marked since Seventy-Five
As the Egyptian first-born,
   Who, joyously alive,
Knew not how soon, how sure, how grim
The night of death awaited him.

Now, silent 'mid our keening,
   Now, cold and dumb as he,
They lie; while through the darkness
   What roaring host goes free?
What nations wake? what peoples cry?
What new device of liberty?

O Ireland broken-hearted,
   O Poland newly-called,
O slain through generations,
   Judah,—were ye unthralled
When, struck with fire no rains could quell
Those heads of admiration fell?

In Time of War

Amen : come also quickly,
  Immortal Death and young,
Where walk we, charged with sorrow,
  Their purposes among :
For their love's sake who brought us in,
Death, be we counted of thy kin :

They, ere that last fulfilment
  And climax of their wars,
Sat in their youth beside thee,
  Thy close familiars :
Yea, with such zeal ensued thine ends,
Servants thou call'dst them not, but friends.

But we—poor exiles—hunger
  Within our plenteous ease
For those hid happy moments
  When he who loves thee sees
Imminent dangers come abroad,
And thee thyself upon his road.

So we behold thee, Master,
  On far interior hills,
Hearing thy thin sweet music,
  The strain that saves and kills,
Calling to solitude and fast,
Until Possession be outcast.

How like a naked beggar,
  My prince, thou travellest !
Who art in Wisdom's chambers
  A high convenient guest.
At Beauty's table art thou fed,
And O thou sleep'st in Love's own bed !

In Time of War

Dull are Delight's best revels
   Until thou bidd'st rejoice ;
And the Nine silent Muses
   Thou touchest into voice ;
Passion—thy foster-son—hath known
No wakening call but thine alone !

How shall we not desire thee,
   We the least sons of Earth ?
O strip us of our garments,
   Encompass us with dearth !
Salt is the food that Plenty brings,
But thou hast healing in thy wings !

Come, master of salvation,
   And coming bring with thee
Zeal, Poverty, and Wisdom,
   Confirmèd Chastity,
Joy, that is dead till thou be nigh,
Laughter and Song and Prophecy !

In Time of War

II. LOVERS TO LOVERS

WHEN peacefully we moved amid your peace,
   What hour foresaw that we should turn ingrate,
And, loath untouched by war to bid war cease,
   Hold you thus severed and discorporate?

Our wills, that dare not break with war's will, thus
   Are made the agents of your sole divorce :
To you the rent, the agony ; to us
   Salvation, hardly tinctured with remorse.

Yet doubt not soon, in some new wrath immersed,
   On us our Lord Love shall avenge your pain,
When, smitten with disaster, we shall thirst
   For consolation,—and shall thirst in vain.

In Time of War

III. ON THE WAY TO SOMERSET

THROUGH the mid counties, shining with their water,
   Sharp as we swung, all labour left behind,
Into the West land and our days of laughter,
   Wholly the great wars vanished from our mind.

Wantage arose, with her battles all of faery,
   Kings half-divine who dammed the sea-swept hordes ;
Bath, with her ghostly walks and gardens airy,
   Bright with her duels and memory of swords.

Dim, as we gazed, grew the little churches, moulded
   But from one myth of all that mythic strain.
—Lo, all abruptly to our sight unfolded,
   Flat lay a wheatfield, under storms of rain.

Then in our hearts we saw the farther water,
   Transports and cruisers, hospitals and mines,
Heard the great guns,—and vanished all our laughter,—
   Where in our wars the rifles guard the lines.

In Time of War

IV. IN ABSENCE

THINK not, although no more you walk
In English roads or with us talk,
That we and English roads are free
From your continual company.

For, since on that last enterprise
Were closed your tired and bloody eyes,
On some new expedition gone,
Though your souls leave our souls alone;

Yet now, those seasons to retrieve
Which they some while were loath to leave,
And by our sharpened sense discerned,
Your bodies are themselves returned:

Or, being held still in their place,
With strong desire turn backward space,
Make England France, and draw us through
To be environed there with you.

So we, 'neath strangers' footsteps, hear
Your heavy marches sounding near;
And in your silent listening post
Are their confusèd noises lost.

To walls and window-curtains cling
Your voices at each breakfasting,
As the cups pass from hand to hand,
Crying for drink in No Man's Land.

In Time of War

Through all the gutters of the town
Your blood—your ghostly blood !—runs down,
Spreads in slow pools, and stains the feet
Of all who cross your ancient street.

On hills and heaths, where once you lay
Reading beneath the hot noonday,
Now if we lie, how near you keep—
But still, but frozen, but asleep !

In Time of War

V. REUNION

PLEASANT companion Sleep, refrain
  While meditation tells
How deep in England once again
  A cherished friendship dwells.

All waves that round this island go
  Now closely us combine,
Since none but English rivers flow
  Between his door and mine.

Now I with him may once again
  Our ancient quest begin ;
By speech the working of his brain
  To me may enter in.

Nor needs there speech if glance meet glance,
  On walks or at the play,
Or anywhere I by good chance
  May meet him any day.

In Time of War

VI. FOR A PIETÀ

SORROW am I, though none has seen my tears.
　　To me for comfort all men's childhood ran ;
To me men's dolour piously uprears
　　This image, where I mourn, not men, but man.
I am that which lives when in your darkest hour
　　Not heroes only, but their hopes, have died.
I am the desolation, and the power
　　Of patience ; I await what shall betide.

Ballade of a Country Day

THE burden of a day of country good :
   From the young morn till afternoon grew late
Over her bright hair May drew up the hood
   Of her dark cloud ; cities grew out of date
   To us, between whom, while we walked or sate,
Sprang the old questions never words make stale,—
   If Love be lord of us or only Fate,
If Sarras be, if Sarras hold the Grail.

The apple and the gorse in Chorley Wood
   Bloomed ; the wide fields stretched wet and desolate ;
And o'er them vanished the quick swallows' brood ;
   Light far off shone through the beech openings strait,
   True and translucent green,—seeming fit mate
For the full colour of that eternal vale,
   To its mid town of Sarras consecrate,
If Sarras be, if Sarras hold the Grail.

Gods have men known of anger and of blood,
   Gods of the north, of tempest, and of hate,
Gods of a happier earth and kindlier mood,
   But whatso God in Sarras doth estate
   Mortality in light, and there await
Our journey's term, to hear our ventures' tale,
   Rejoices in those fields of broad debate,
If Sarras be, if Sarras hold the Grail.

Ballade of a Country Day

ENVOY

Heroes, innumerable perils wait,
  Earth and the lesser heavens have sworn our bale,
Pledge we anew to meet by Sarras' gate,
  If Sarras be, if Sarras hold the Grail.

Ballade of Travellers

NAMES are written on maps unrolled
  Of shires and cities, great books are lined
With titles sounding as far bells tolled
  In hearts of romance on a veering wind;
  Yet when the homes of those words we find
How is their wizardry all undone!
  Hardly we say, as we walk resigned,
Through the whole world's towns is the Free Town one.

In a seven-nights' space is a new town old,
  Seven mornings teach us the ways that wind
To quay or market, to farm or wold,
  And lost are the ways that lie behind.
  Lucent no more are the bricks, or blind
Are we, and with memories overrun;
  We pine abroad as at home we pined:
Through the whole world's towns is the Free Town one.

Ports and the deep-sea boats they hold,
  High roads where vessels of traffic grind,
Hamlets which lanes or moors enfold,—
  None to the heart shall contentment bind:
  One city alone to men is kind,
That is seen and seen not, and kept of none,
  Yet allwhere hath ever to earth inclined:
Through the whole world's towns is the Free Town one.

Ballade of Travellers

ENVOY

Prince, whether we dwell in a street assigned
  Or wander under a changing sun,
This be the token that stills our mind :
  Through the whole world's towns is the Free Town one.

Ghosts

IF that which earth from heaven divides
  Were softly all removed,
And I at the next corner met
  With you whom once I loved,

No friendship 'twixt your eyes and mine
  Should suddenly revive,—
Who, charged with heaven in all your veins,
  In a new London thrive.

Along this doubly-pavèd street
  Though you should walk with me,
No right communion should attend
  On that epiphany.

Wiser than such estrangèd sight
  To see your shadows loom
Along this shadowed road by night,
  Gloom visioned upon gloom :

While exhalations of the street
  And vapours of my mind
Mingle within the past, and drift
  Upon a ghostly wind.

By such vague symbols of your truth
  Be your great spirits known,
Till to my tread this pavement yields
  Its firmer under-stone.

Ghosts

But O as now in that high town
   Your souls of courage live,
Save me from darkness when my own
   I into judgement give.

Speak to the ministry of Fate
   Lest, when this world dissolves,
Some vaporous and ghostly cloud
   My fleeing soul involves.

Your heavenly conversation turn
   Some while in aid of me,
That I may now, in these dark ways,
   Glimpse of your city see ;

And, though our parted loves no more
   Shall grace with grace requite,
These sacramental roads may be
   With your true presence bright.

To Michal: After a Vigil

LAST night I slept not
  Close in your bed,
Nor could I cherish
  There your dark head:
O, was I found in your dream?

Dreams, none can rule them;
  I, more content,
Sought you and found you
  Where I was bent:
O, was an ending to dream!

That body's beauty,
  Where your dreams coast,
Knew I and neared I,
  Hid in the Host,—
O, else was beauty but dream!—

In the transparent
  Small fragile cake
Wherethrough our Lord Love
  Almost doth break:
O, else was body but dream!

There, to true matter
  Eyes half-unlatched,
Through the night-season
  For you I watched:
O, then I knew what was dream!

To Michal : After a Vigil

Here to my vision
　　Move you, cloud-swirled
By all the mist blown
　　Through the dim world :
O, is it vision or dream ?

In the True Body,
　　Lo, your true face
Looked to behold me,
　　There, beyond space :
O, was an ending to dream !

There, where all perfect
　　Matter is stored,
In our true bodies
　　Met we, Adored !
O, but we sink now to dream

House-hunting

I

In the high town which is eternity,
    The plotted comprehension of all souls,
    Through which the all-tributaried river rolls
Waters of peace, and spreads communicably
In wells, canals, fountains, and middle sea ;
    Where Love, in commerce 'twixt his settled poles,
    God and the people, mightily controls
And is controlled by spirits just and free :

There have all towns and times of towns their place,
    Being modes of our interior city, fit,
Each at its special knot of Time and Space,
    For some immortal to eternize it,
    Meet for some soul to find by heavenly wit
And to inhabit in that town of grace.

II

In that eternal town what shall we find,
    What house of the whole world, modern or antique,
    Best after our lives' pattern ? shall we seek
Broad-knowledged neighbourhoods with our own kind,—
Felt here by men as the Athenian mind ?
    Or the Carthusians' solitary, bleak,
    And Gothic height ? or, found for that too weak,
Some quiet street, here in Dutch towns divined ?

Or shall our joyous spirits cross some bridge
    Of tenderness into past passion, set
        For ever in that true world, and regain
        The county where our lives were truest, lane
    Of Hertfordshire, cottage of Somerset,
Or—more familiar—Hampstead's road and ridge ?

House-hunting

III

HAPPY that town ! happy its citizens !
  Most happy we if we inhabit, Fair,
  On any windy height or sunny square,
In God's immediate presence or true men's :
But also that full stream through swamps and fens
  Labours and twists its way ; O what if there
  We by the force of our past wills repair
To feverish hovels or infectious dens ?

O if, diseased by the world's lust and blind
  To those great walks and avenues, we come
Into the huts and tenements man's mind
  Here by Zambesi builds or Thames,—the sum
And dwelling of our foul lives and unkind,
  In the last haunts of Pandemonium !

IV

OR you with Love being mightily content,
  The sickness done which your light present sin
  Shall at that change bring on till, pale and thin,
You are renewed with heavenly nourishment,—
That hot and scarfing malady quite spent,
  Shall you, some household of his choice within,
  With him new travel and new toil begin,
Nor glance at dogs on their own mischief bent ?

Nor know that I, so hidden from your eyes,
  Still, to my own, am prisoned by that place
    Where once I, loosing all my lust, my power
    To stamp eternity upon an hour,
Chose my full lot,—nor there shall recognize
  Your fragrant head, your glad eternal face ?

Celestial Cities

I saw no temple therein.

WHEN our translated cities
    Are joyous and divine,
And through the streets of London
    The streets of Sarras shine,
When what is hid in London
    Doth then in Sarras show,
And we in that new township
    The ancient highways know,
Though the bricks sing together
    In those celestial walls,
Shall we not long, o'er Ludgate,
    To see the dome of Paul's?

When we shall hear—how gladly !—
    The general shout declare
That up Cheapside his pageant
    Conveys the young Lord Mayor,
When all applause salutes him,
    Man chosen among men,
By proof of former friendship
    Known to each citizen,
Though in his streets of freedom
    Our happy souls confer,
Shall we not miss the towers,
    The gates, of Westminster?

There shall our little churches
    To open squares be turned,
And daylight shine for ever
    Where once the candles burned:

Celestial Cities

But ah, by Thames the Temple
    Untempled there shall be;
No more shall rise by London Bridge
    Saint Mary Overy;
Saint Martin's-in-the-Fields shall pass,
    Saint Clement Danes come down,
And silent be the bells of dawn
    From Kew to Kentish Town!

Shall we not muse a little
    On how we talked afar
Of Roman and Byzantine
    And Perpendicular?
When the world's dreams and visions
    Immanuel fulfils,
How bare shall lie before us
    These abbeyed vales and hills!
When we shall look from Sarras
    Across her pleasant shire,
And see a thousand hamlets
    But not a single spire!

Ballad of Material Things

THE devil walked by Hell Gate, that opens upon earth,
And saw a cloud of conflict around the house of birth,
And highly mourned Beelzebub, that holy place within
To see so much of courtesy and such a lack of sin.

For three gates give on Mansoul, by two the spirits come,
Tribunes of Sarras, tyrants of Pandemonium ;
But by the other portal, too narrow for such wings,
The unborn souls of manhood come to material things.

Then answered the prince Moloch : ' There lacks not, O our
        lord,
Battle and skill for battle in stratagem and sword,
And companies of valour and generals therefor ;
And all Mansoul is riotous with noise of civil war.

' And often are men traitors, but yet for all our pains
The oldest of their buildings untaken yet remains :
By Sarras' portal Michael is fighting desperately,
But O to win the third gate, the lowest of the three !

' For there the lanes and alleys all thick and twisted lie,
So close the house roofs lean across we cannot see the sky,
And there, when all the rest is lost, still flies the flag of
        earth,
And there man's strength renews itself, by that low gate of
        birth.

' If thou wilt rise and take it, O star of victory,
No refuge from our conquest in all mankind shall be ;
The Burning Heart of Dante before our shafts shall fail,
The Daffodils of Wordsworth shall be of no avail.'

Ballad of Material Things

Then mightily the devil rose to seize the gate of earth,
Around it through the city he set his lines of dearth,
And all about the universe began to run and peer
To force that gate by violence and break its bolts by fear.

On baffled wings of anger, if he might enter in
This gatehouse of man's body and turn it into sin,
He sought as high as Lucifer, but higher still those towers
Were hidden in the night of God and armed with maiden
    powers.

With closed wings downward sank he through fundamental
    seas
To find its lowest stonework amid primaeval trees,
But still the waves beat on it and in the lowest night
Its walls impenetrable stood and armed with maiden might.

Then back he turned to Mansoul and passed to join the
    strife,
And underneath his charges fainted the breath of life ;
Until before its battlements his trumpet call was blown,
And thrice he dashed against it and thrice was overthrown.

'O what art thou to foil me,' the devil cried to it,
'When I have seized man's spirit and poisoned all his wit,
And hope is trampled under me and charity is dead?'
And lightly all the gatehouse replied to him and said :

'Though thou shalt take the city, Beelzebub my foe,
Belfry and cellar bloodily, yet, me to overthrow,
Needs must thou set some ambush to gain the way of flesh,
Thy disincarnate powers in manhood to immesh.

'Go, find some maid to love thee, the portal that sufficed
For entrance to my warder shall serve for Antichrist ;

Ballad of Material Things

Softly shalt thou be born in her, and when the months are
run
Thou shalt be one with matter as he my lord is one.

' But now the law within me outstands your petards wild ;
I that am burnt and blackened shall never be defiled,
Whose bulwarks out to earthward are firm on Godhead
stayed,
Whose arch to heaven is rounded in the secrets of a maid.'

Then surging from those portals the mind of Wordsworth
drew
Immortal strength from woods and hills, and undefeated
flew
The Burning Heart of Dante, and all of matter strove
To aid the arms of Mansoul in nature and in love.

Dialogue between the Republic and the Apostasy

The Voice of the Republic

To all the nations, provinces, and towns,
  Hamlets and huts,—to all Earth's populace,
Serfdoms or synods, parliaments or crowns,
    Be greeting and be grace.

None hath beheld me, yet hath never man
  Shaped with his peers a wall of government
But I was that diviner artisan
    Who spake with his intent.

All civic hungers have in me their scope
  Who of all cities am the purposed Name;
I in men's changing hopes am that one hope
    Which hath myself for aim.

Of my own will I bind myself in walls,
  Sink in foundations and in towers grow high,
Of my own will I stand, and no stone falls,
    There is no town but I.

The Voice of the Apostasy

Hast thou forgot, O City overproud,
  Me, than all things save thee more ancient? I,
Who to my will thy strength have ever bowed,
    Deny thee and defy.

C 2   (35)

Dialogue between the Republic

Oft as thou hurlest into act anew,
   Art within time law and a liberty,
I twist, I break, I perjure, I undo,
    Thou fall'st to tyranny.

Thou hast not, O fair town republican,
   Shaped thyself ever in the bounds of space,
But there hath grown a traitor to that plan,
    A foe against that place.

I of thy fountains drink, I walk in thee,
   One stone thou lay'st and with the next I rise,—
I, Pandemonium, breaking up thy free
    Town with my leaguered spies.

The Voice of the Republic

Thy warfare O mine enemy, I know
   In men and towns upon their end in me,
To love and equal brotherhood a foe,
    A foe to liberty.

Yet, howsoe'er keen, thy created eyes
   Flag in the vistas of the infinite,
None but myself can know my enterprise
    In the clear whole of it.

No spade hath digged, trowel nor mortar joins
   My bricks, nor measures my walls' period ;
For, as a son born of his father's loins,
    Perfect I spring from God.

Thou seest me not, thou hear'st my voice afar ;
   City on city against me thou break'st down ;
While, quicker than thy diligence can mar,
    I rise in town on town.

and the Apostasy

I, to the utmost height of making, God,
  Yet in the depth of all the made am man,
Heaven beyond heaven, clod in crumbling clod,
  Crowned yet republican.

The Voice of the Apostasy

Count up thy ruins through a million years,
  Since Chanoch, man's blood first by man being shed,
Arose, of hatred edified and fears,
  And based upon the dead.

Through all lost ages count thy embers quenched,
  Since men, enlarged into blood-brotherhood,
Yet in their family were split and trenched
  Round greater needs than food.

Since all thy past with broken towns is strewn,
  What final city hop'st thou yet to build?
What site shall serve for it? what stone unhewn?
  What architect? what guild?

The Voice of the Republic

What canst thou know of death, even death, my foe?
  Before time was or any towns began,
Utter destruction did I undergo
  Ere I was safe for man.

Then God in earthquake tore me, all the hills
  Where I Jerusalem am founded shook,
My river ceased, and from my water-mills
  No flour that day he took:

My bulwarks crashed, my palaces were rent,
  And my foundations opened to the air,
Dragons and thieves through all my body went,—
  Wert thou not also there?

Dialogue between the Republic

Or art thou deaf to rumours which o'errun
    The earliest pales man round his altars built,
Of skies made black, divinities undone,
    And of a god's blood spilt?

From such annihilation I arose,
    My breaches shut, my highways re-illumed;
And on eternal conquest I repose,
    To surety re-assumed.

The Voice of the Apostasy

City of boasts!   Yet if thou art indeed
    Aught more than dream, sprung within man's sick mind
Brooding upon the infinite, hear me plead,
    Blind, for my brethren blind.

Lo here the poor, the sacrificed, the maimed:
    All is within thine ending; end it thou!
If thou eternally art Justice named,
    Content them! fashion now

Some swift and sudden miracle to bring
    Peace to thy poor: why wilt thou have them die?
Thy law and men's laws work their suffering,—
    Redeem, heal, satisfy!

How canst thou watch thy folk to such death come,
    Couched in a bitter world, on rough rocks fed,—
Hopelessness, hunger, battle, martyrdom?
    Turn thou their stones to bread!

The Voice of the Republic

Well, O Apostasy, it fits thy mood
    Such satisfaction for my folk to win,
Who so by pretext of immediate good
    Still temptest man to sin.

and the Apostasy

Men slay? I bear; are slain? yet I endure.
  No easy justice bring I nor quick peace;
Misers and conquerors torment my poor,
    I make them not to cease.

For since some huge gorilla mumbled 'I',
  And back the whole creation thundered 'thou',
The freedom of my sons I ratify,
    Nor their choice disallow.

No spirit's littlest deed but must long while
  Work on, must infinitely breed in me,
Who only can atone and reconcile
    In my eternity.

The Voice of the Apostasy

Therefore if these thy folk shall be downtrod
  Till to thy weakness the strong heart be slave,
The miserly grow liberal as God,
    Long shalt thou take to save!

O but for shame's sake shorten thou the time!
  Convert the rich since thou wilt feed no poor!
Turn the proud hopes which think through power to climb
    To some imperial floor.

Earth's wounded loves beneath them fall and bleed,
  Only since Love himself will never show;
If thou art Love, be seen! thereon indeed
    Shall all things loveward flow.

No more thy foes shall mock thy advent then,
  Nor thy true sons at thy slow date repine;
If thou art the Jerusalem of men,
    Fair City, rise and shine!

Dialogue between the Republic

Show but thyself, thou need'st not to command!
  Then shall all living know and spring to thee,
Then will I give all things into thy hand,
  I and my friends with me.

The Voice of the Republic

If all the kingdoms of the world were mine,
  Doubtless their emperor the kings should know,
Before me, their souls' Suleiman, incline
  Abased: I choose not so.

I, a fair town, free and republican,
  Graced by my citizens electively,
Who to all men am native, being man,
  Am equal, being free,—

I as an equal amid equals move;
  Am to each heart but one 'mid many a choice,
Nor with persuasion beyond any love
  Entreat him for his voice.

Chooses he? I at ending shine, a God.
  Refuses? But a dream I pass away.
Accepts? The heavens shall be his native sod.
  Rejects? He treads but clay.

O as too soon I move not to my end,
  So never with magniloquence I woo,
I, Love, who only can a man befriend
  If he be glad thereto.

The Voice of the Apostasy

Have then thy choice! no need is mine to shrink
  From the aeonian strife thy will prepares,
Which man endures, caught on that battle's brink,
  And miserably shares.

and the Apostasy

Now busy over hearth and aqueduct,
  Now lost in bloody quarrels o'er his plan,
Now bold to build, now of all boldness sucked,
    Behold thy creature, man.

Still false, still changing his immediate past,
  And constant only to apostasy,
This is the mind, O City, where thou hast
    Thy sole reality.

But—his endeavours broken—by and by
  He to the slime wherein his race began
Shall slip again, and perish ; man shall die,
    And thou shalt die with man.

The Voice of the Republic

Well hast thou marked man's bloody star, my foe,
  Mocked his defeats, twisted his victories !
Only one thing nor he nor thou canst know,—
    How swiftly I increase !

Each perfidy is fuel to my fire
  Of wrath, each loyalty my mercy feeds ;
That double passion drew him from the mire
    And to salvation speeds.

Each truth, each untruth, waking deep in me,
  Quickens my spirit ; almost is time spanned :
Feel'st thou not, feel'st not, O mine enemy,
    My hour, my hour at hand ?

Mercy and wrath within man's holiest mind
  Are piled and imminent ; thou, quite outcast,
Incapable of me, shalt only find
    No cities more to blast.

(41)

The Republic and the Apostasy

That hour will I fulfil man's liberties,
   His imperfections with perfection close,—
An hour which, save my chosen, none foresees,
   Nor, save my Father, knows ;

When this opaque world shall by me be lit,
   And I be manifest,—not to destroy,
Not to destroy, but to transfigure it
   With uncreated joy.

Then visibly shall I be bound in walls,
   Sink in foundations and in towers grow high,
Then shall I stand and shine while no stone falls,
   There shall be naught but I.

At the Gates

BECAUSE no man has slandered me
Or wrought me evil, with what plea

Shall I approach to enter in,
Where they who suffered under sin

And their oppressors have forgiven,
Make a sweet concord thorough heaven?

I who have spent my time at ease,
Untouched of man's injustices,

Shall find then how my comfort lets
That I should say *Forgive my debts*

As I forgive all owed to me.
Ah, fair souls, purged by love, can ye

Endure that I too should belong—
I who have wrought, not suffered, wrong,—

To your companionship? for there
'Tis your forgiveness makes you fair.

O let me pass, though I shall walk
Least in your city, and your talk

Shall never join, who only live
To take your pardon, not to give.

But what if I have injured one
Whose way so far from yours hath run

At the Gates

That he eternally puts on
Mysterious disunion

From God, your chosen?   Him no praye
For pardon from me waiting there

Shall reach or pierce, and how shall I
Enter, while his avenging cry

Against my past and me shall come
Inward from Pandemonium?

Ah, lord Love, grant my sins may be
Wrought all against thy saints and thee!

On the German Emperor

PARDON, you ruined bodies of our war,
  That we less wrath than consolation find
In thinking upon that dire emperor,
  Who loosed all mankind's pride upon mankind
For since he bears our sins and we bear his,—
  So dread the cousinship of flesh and bone,—
This bloody spectacle none other is
  Than Love in us betrayed and quite undone.
O dark design of comfort!—Him, we know,
  Love turns to meet and in quick arms to fold;
We too, 'tis seen then, may be greeted so,
  Us too Love's pardon may be swift to hold,—
    Pardon we dared not trust till lo, it showers
    Upon this deed, which is but like to ours.

To Michal : On Forgiveness

WHEN fault of madness or of sloth
Has wrecked our often plighted troth,
And all your angers, justly moved,
Lighten upon this earth you loved,
How soon they sleep ! how swiftly new,
Ere yet my trouble turns to you,
Your tenderness prepares my rest
Upon your all-forgiving breast !

More proudly, for some evil chance
Of harmful-harmless ignorance,
Or some pure foolishness of thought
Wherein my good intent is caught,
You, pricked with the unmeant offence,
Demand a courteous penitence,
Before those eyes, wherein I live,
Caution, admonish, and forgive.

But how your beauty knows to shine
In pomp, how consciously divine
At times you let your pardons fall
Where has been found no fault at all ;
And your tyrannical desire
Contrite repentance doth require
From love, which willingly hath striven,—
Only to have itself forgiven.

Politics

ONE, indivisible, and free,
    Notes of the only True !—
O Christian creed of deity
    She wholly does indue !
O high republican decree,
    Refusing prince and shah !
One, indivisible, and free,
    The triple formula !

Bourbon and Brunswick, Valmy done,
    Heard a great silence tell
The first free nation risen, one
    And indivisible :
One God the doctors of the schools,
    With Rabbi and Imam,
Teach to my heart one mistress rules
    In a transfigured calm.

But ah, what war that land betides
    Who does her clerks and hinds
Neglect, while tyranny divides
    Her many million minds ;
Nor in such blessèd union moves
    As in her passion she ;
As in their quick creation Love's
    Complicit Trinity.

Politics

Happy the people who, once freed,
  Equal and plighted all,
Afford to each interior need
  And each exterior call
Such quick access as prayer controls
  To God, such quick reply
As to one soul from one sweet soul's
  Perpetual charity.

Alas how long ere, sorrow-wise,
  The heart of England feel
And in her politic devise
  That sacred commonweal,—
One, indivisible, and free,
  Notes of the only True,
Taught, Fair, to all in deity,
  And taught to me in you !

First Love

WILT thou regret I never wooed
  As hastier lovers will,—
Who, too incredulous of mood,
  Attended for thee still?

Deeply my half-reluctant sense
  Doubted its own delight,
Till, closing all that high suspense,
  I dared believe in sight!

But if I long considered, Fair,
  How love at all could be,
Much more will I reject despair
  And keep this faith in thee.

I will of doubt make such an art
  That no dismay shall move
Sufficient bitterness of heart
  For unbelief in love;

And still of death incredulous
  Till death, outworn, shall die,
My curious mind shall enter thus
  Into eternity.

Love is Lost

LOVE is lost and gone astray :
    O for pity !
He has found a moonlit way
    From the city.
Where shall we seek him ?   O say, O say !

We have searched through every lane
    Where the lovers
Walk in twilight : but our pain
    Ne'er discovers
That god, that glory, yet are we fain !

Have ye climbed unto the meads
    Where her races
Cynthia, ever vestal, leads ?
    Marked his traces
Far from the highway, through grass and reeds ?

Know ye not how tales aver
    His famed mother
Venus was his kidnapper ?
    And another
(O vestal Cynthia !) despoiled by her ?

In Venus' town he beaten was
    For his longing ;
Wherefore he escapèd has
    From that wronging.
Ye shall behold him, where the maids pass.

Love is Lost

Watch, till Cynthia go by !
  Ye shall find him :
But in her chaste company
  Naught shall bind him.
Call him, beseech him, but go not nigh !

Incidents

FLOWER-DECKED table set for tea,
  Cake and bread-and-butter,
All the casual courtesy
  That her sweet lips utter,
O the flames, the little flames!
O the strong fire burning!

Candles in the candlesticks
  Bright on cup and platter,
Gossip and deep talk that mix
  In an evening's chatter,
O the pools, the little pools!
O the full flood running!

Service to our daily lot
  With what gayness tendered,
Deeds and words and glances shot
  With her love once rendered,
O her acts, her little acts!
O her brooding passion!

Return

HEART, why labourest thou?
                                    I pant
With the pressure of my want.

Was not unto thee, alone
Last night lying, thy need shown?

O not till to her I go.

Why then dost thou move so slow,
Heart? why labourest thou?
                                    Alas,
What could bring me to this pass
But to feel how near now she
Sighs: O love, I wait for thee?

Why art thou distressed?
                                    O peace!
I am faint with the increase
Of her neighbourhood, I die
If she help not speedily.

Her dark Eyes sparkle

HER dark eyes sparkle,
Whate'er our way,
On all about her
The times display,
On grate or window
Or passer-by,
So quick and gaily
And watchfully :

While mine are brooding
Upon that show,
Heavily lying
And moving slow ;
They gain no tincture
(Ashamed and dull)
From all earth's beauties
Most worshipful.

Sweet eyes, remember
This slothful pair,
Teaching them duty
Everywhere
To sight and knowledge
Of things and men,
But when they meet you
O hold them then.

Four Sonnets

I

When, playing through the world, my song puts claim
  To station with Love's peers and guild-masters,
And they perchance make question of thy name,
  Saying : 'What she is this thy voice prefers?'
To them my song : 'Ah, when my master goes
  In twilight, careless of the elvish ring,
Or gnomic dance, or faery, and bestows
  Trouble in sighs, more deep than rhyme can sing,—
O when his voice, though fain it be to find
  A breath more insubstantial than the air,
An auditor more secret than the wind,
  Yearns yet to cry, lest no more it can bear,—
    Though earth be still as night in Eden were,
    He cannot speak,—her name 's too close to her!'

II

All toilful words, all tale of arduous hours
  Can nowise sum the greatness of the care
Which hath safe-compassed, by laborious powers,
  Me, such love's son and quite desertless heir.
All service that my years profess they bring
  Through tenderness of that familiar grace,
And what hast thou to set against this thing
  Save the imperious mandate of thy face?
Guilty receiver of that stolen sweet,
  The store of love I from my mother drew
Throughout my nonage—O unmeant deceit!—
  To what an end nor she nor I then knew,
    How canst thou with such unperturbèd heart
    Meet her, who of that sweet had all the smart

Four Sonnets

III

HALF nun thou seem'st and half a bacchanal,
   Devout, yet ruddied in the dancing whirl:
O from what cloister or what carnival
   Grew'st thou for me incarnate and a girl?
And still in obscure shadows of thine eyes
   A crouching fierceness threats the path of man
I feel through all my limbs the savage rise,
   Grappling with thee in strife barbarian.
And little there should daily courtesy
   Make truce, or reason put an end to hate,
Except thy grave look push the farther plea:
   'We were converted unto love of late.'
      Thy silver trumpets through me lead thy van;
      But O beneath, hark the wild pipes of Pan!

IV

O TO what laws in kisses we assent
   When our rejoicing wills in them accord!
Severity our fathers underwent
   Blooms here in beauty for a late reward.
Set man's deeds by, and only think with me
   What throngs those natural influences slew
Which here put on a fair hypocrisy
   And hide their past of massacre in you.
The stuff whereof these lovely limbs are wrought
   Was lava once, a bursting tidal wave,
Or berries with untested poison fraught,
   Or desert sand,—but every way a grave.
      Thus I in you deliberately embrace
      Nature, and all her warfare on our race.

After Marriage

I

WHY, Fairest, in such deep delay
Was thy chief fairness hid away?
Ah, sweet procrastinator, thou
Hast kept the good wine until now!

Graces, I see, thou well couldst spare,
Concealed the central grace they bare;
The play begun, thy courtship moods
At loveliest were but gay preludes.

Then show'dst thou a fair land to hold
And strewn with love's alluvial gold;
But, now thy deeper veins are mined,
To uses of exchange assigned,

With some alloy of duty in 't
Love issues daily from thy mint;
While to our new-built barns and stores
Grain from rich fields of beauty pours.

Yet though our hearts each other till,
Such increase is mere miracle,
So much of harvest-tide our Sun
Condensed into few days or none.

After Marriage

For when, bewildered and in tears,
We waited the ensuing years,
Clinging in terror to the past,
God's Mother saw us there aghast;

And with a word did Him prepare
To fill the waterpots; cast, Fair,
That song about him also—'Thou
Hast kept the good wine until now!'

II

No watcher saw when first you moved
O'er my dispersèd heart, beloved,
Nor in that unruled chaos' storm
Beheld your image taking form.

Long hid within me did I hold
The gospel your bright forehead told,
And secret to my proper want
Preserved your eyes' new covenant.

But now, since, opened and exposed,
Those vows profound in marriage closed,
And all my public life is shown
Yours utterly and yours alone:

Why have you yielded your control
Upon that most interior soul,
Which now, as ere you first drew near,
Is shaken with excess of fear?

After Marriage

Your spirit, with your beauty edged,
To final government alleged
My heart's surrender late to be :—
Whence issues this new destiny ?

What advent of what farther law
Bids you, my Fair, from me withdraw
From me, dispersed in ancient pain
And into chaos plunged again ?

Loving and Loved

LOVING and loved, myself last night I laid
    To rest in peace,
Nor knew that very night how destiny
    Should come to me,
And I should rise up outlawed and afraid,
    And quiet cease.

In dream my love and I walked in a wood,
    Misty but fair ;
And by us suddenly ran a great crowd,
    In terror loud,
By some fierce creature of the wild pursued,
    Lion or bear.

In dream I left my love and feared and fled ;
    And all the folk
Faded ; alone I ran with panting breath ;—
    Left her to death
And ran, but after me the fierce thing sped,—
    And I awoke.

I woke, but all the terror surged anew
    Within my heart,
In premonition of an hour to be
    When I shall flee
From her most need, fail from her when a crew
    Of dangers start.

To Michal : On Brushing her Hair

BENEATH the brushes, from that low pale brow
The lustrous dark hair falls aside to show
A face which some pre-Raphaelite should have loved
And magnified when sighing passion moved
In his coiled quatrains of luxurious verse,
Or where his patterns, glint on glint, rehearse
Their turned refrain : what other poets praised
So well such cheeks and perfect eyelids, raised
From such deep eyes of glamour ?
                                    As they close,
Beneath the soothing and swift passages,
A sudden transmutation quite undoes
That verse : divine Victoria is dead ;
In that short lip are tracked new poesies,
New rhythms along that small preposterous head

Experiments

I. TRAFFIC

THESE shapes of brown and black painted horses,
These bright dabs on the street
Like motor-buses,—
If I stood in front of them, would they crush me?
Surely not: I should find
They were cut out of paper, cardboard, or tinted metal,
They and their riders and all the hats and parasols on them,
Thin, almost two-dimensioned,
And would either lean up against me or bounce over me —
Bounce, I think.

Experiments

II. ANARCHY

How dull it is
Always to do just the same thing with words,
Always to fashion them into ordered sentences,
After thought
Of their sounds, associations, purposes, et cetera,
Because they mean something,
And these meanings must explode together into others,
Spreading meaning, always meaning,
Over the unfortunate earth.

(Not only poets,
But all of us do it every day, miserable talkers!)

If one only could pile words up in a heap,
Or make carpets of them,
Or dig holes in the longer ones,
Or put them in a farmyard to grub about with the pigs!
But no, they must mean something,
And alas,
How little worth while it is to mean anything,
And how useless to try!

Also (O how desirable!)
If one could only destroy some words altogether,

(63)

Experiments

Them
And their substantival, adjectival, adverbial, and compound
    derivatives
To infinity ;
Living happily ever afterwards
In a world free from such words as *whisky* or *snigger*.

Experiments

III. IMPOSSIBILITY

I WAS walking past
The Tube train carriage, when it began to move ;
And before I knew what I wanted
It had slipped away from me.

So now I can never catch up the other end of it,
And never till then
Had I known what an impossibility was.

To see it disappearing,
And my purpose for ever frustrated,
Was almost more than I could bear,
For I had supposed
I should pass it before it began to move.

But that one carriage is purified
From my rivalry for ever, undefiled by my parallel walk,
Clean.

On Walt Whitman's 'Song of Myself'

LOUD, loud he calls, loud tells us how he calls
   Thieves, harlots, poets, packmen, millionaires;
   How he is brother to them all, and fares
Exultantly through earth, cheerily bawls
An inventory of humankind: he falls
   With the weak (he cries), and climbs celestial stairs
   With saints; to storms and soft spring winds he bares
A head no fear or inexperience shawls.

As greatly one long since in England loved
   His fellows; with as deep fraternity
     Fathomed their hearts, until he seemed to bring
A world into the world: but himself moved
   Silently then, and now as shadowy
     As Ossian, or some tumulus-memoried king.

Briseis

THE footfalls of the parting Myrmidons
    And countercries of leaguer and of town
    Are hushed behind her as the silks drop down ;
Alone she stands and wonderingly cons
Heads circleted with gold or helmed with bronze ;
    Higher her eyes, from crown to loftier crown,
    Creep, till they fall, nigh blasted, at the frown
Of Argos,—throned in his pavilions,
And mid his captains wrathfully aware
  How the plague smites the host, how by the sea
    Beyond the ships, with vengeful prayer and oath,
    Rages the young Achilles ; of whose wrath,
  Innocent, ignorant, a captive, she
Sees but the dropped staff on the voided chair.

Helen in the Chamber of Deiphobus

BLACK is the night and moonless is the sky ;
   No star above pierces the heaven's dark ;
   Below, no camp-fires, braziers on no bark
The sleepy Trojan sentinels espy :
Within, where Priam's youngest son laid by
   His armour, seems the long war's final spark
   To flicker and expire.   Helen, to hark
What footstep, through the casement heard, draws nigh,
Leans, sword on helm and helm on greaves close wrapped
   From glint or clangour in her cloak of wool,
By prone Deiphobus, on whom entrapped
   The central swords of battle shall burn full
Presently, in that errand's blaze whereon
Sinon is now with secret swiftness gone.

To Michal meditating a new Costume

THOUGH experts make to-day the dress
That shall enclose your loveliness,
And, marvellous in art, contrive
To make your beauty more alive,
They have no stuff and cannot sew
The clothes to suit you when you go
Among all ladies fair and dear
To keep the May of our New Year.

Then all the world and heaven shall see
Your pleasant gown of chastity;
Your hat, in that celestial weather,
Shall have a close-trimmed phoenix' feather,
Or, gathered from that joyous Spring,
A rose-bud, real and undying,—
As fashion still perchance be there
Of love or wisdom: you shall bear
A parasol of sweet concern
For others, lest the Sun should burn
Too dark your brilliant countenance,
And dazzle your sun-borrowed glance;
But, since no storms are there to heed,
Within those walks you shall not need,
Nor lose, umbrellas any more:

To Michal meditating a new Costume

You will not trouble much the store
Of jewels, as you do not here,
Only your finger still shall bear
The single glowing ruby of
Your passionate immortal love.

A comb of duty in your hair
Shall prove your diligence and care
To have your beauty dressed aright
Only to give our host delight ;
Your handkerchief of laces, which
The world's delight in you made rich,
You then must carry for display,
Since upon our high feast of May
Shall be no tears to wipe away ;
Your gloves of smooth discretion shall
Suit well that place magnifical,
And on that sward your feet shall be
Compactly shod with industry.

For a Cathedral Door

SHALL I come here alone for praise and prayer,
   Even to this famous house and wonderful,
And quite forget where else I do repair?
   O let none think that I am grown so dull!
O no, I have a house more marvellous,
   More shining, mortared with diviner stuff,
Which to consider is more dangerous :
   Almost my love for me is church enough.
But lest even in devotion I grow proud,
   Seeing I reach heaven by so pure a stair,
Meet is it that I be in this place bowed,
   Confessing each religious hath his fair.
     Yet here be these lines fixed ; let none remove
     This praise of Love's house from the house of Love.

To Michal: On Disputing outside Church

CHAFE not, madonna, that the foe could cheat
  This moment from thy heart outworn and slack.
  In the main battle's brunt thou didst not lack :
Think what huge field of conquest or defeat
This hour was closed ; if, breathless from that heat,
  Thou felt'st some little loss, some slight attack,
  Some dart launched at thy less-defended back,
It cannot win again the spirit's seat.

There if thou fail'dst (as, sure, thou couldst not !), more
And greater guilt comes soon, to sorrow o'er :
  But rather now all's conquered ! thou shalt feel,
A day, a sennight hence, what tempters fled
From those hot prayers. Thy foot there crushed his head,
  Smile if the dragon's claw here tore thy heel.

Invitation to Early Communion

WAKE, majesty! the night clouds break,
    The world becomes alive,
The sleepy priests and servers wake
    To hear their clocks ring five:
The motions of your mouth new-kissed
    Bestir your mind of sleep:
Up, Fair! last night we pledged a tryst
    To-day must see us keep.

Up! ere the next half-hour shall pass,
    You, newly gowned and shod,
Must with quick hands before your glass
    Prepare to meet your God,
Who, launched in courses of his laws,—
    How fails my heart with fear!—
Now to that assignation draws
    Inexorably near!

Vexilla regis prodeunt,
    The double banners move
Before one altar to confront,—
    Twice-manifested Love!
Your face, your soul, a double veil,
    Are closely wrapped round him
Who now, in yon material grail,
    Is nearer, yet more dim!

Invitation to Early Communion

One look, one kiss! and then to prayer:
 He bids no more delay
Who in our hearts long since, my Fair,
 Himself prepared his way.
Disjoin and come, lest we be missed!
 Come, holy and adored!
Day breaks, and Love is at the tryst:
 Come forth to meet your Lord!

At the 'Ye that do truly'

Now are our prayers divided, now
Must you go lonelily, and I :
For penitence shall disallow
Communion and propinquity.

Together we commandments heard,
Paid tithes together and professed :
Now mourns a solitary word
Where solitary deeds transgressed.

Averted be that head of grace,
And turned those melancholy eyes
To weep, within a narrow place
And shadow of iniquities.

Farewell ! we may no more be kind,
Nor either ease the other's breath ;
Death shall our marriage vows unbind,
Death, and this sharp foretaste of death.

Farewell ! before this hour is done
We shall have met or missed, my dear,
In a remoter union,
But now the solitudes are here.

On leaving Church

THE ceremonial gestures end,
    The trancèd limbs are free,
Fast, fast our rising hearts ascend
    From sinking Deity.
The Greater Mysteries recede,
    Again the Lesser rise,
And, furnished for our daily need,
    Appear the earthly skies.

Now wait the substituted doles,—
    Our ritual falling mute,—
For this diviner food of souls,
    Itself half-substitute :
The sacred ministers are gone,
    The royal banners furled,
And we, our dullness putting on,
    Are left unto the world.

Yet at our table, even then,
    Of common food, what grace
Adorns that outer world of men,
    In your possessèd face ;
Where, watching in the Holy Ghost,
    I see our Lord fulfil
His outer dwelling, yea, almost
    He there is visible.

On leaving Church

Himself he here to us imparts,
    But there himself he shows :
Be watchful, eyes ! be mindful, hearts !
    As the church-doors unclose.
The noises of the world's concern
    And the high sun break through :
I rise, I genuflect, I turn
    To breakfast, and to you !

Commentaries—I

In the beginning God created the heavens and the earth.
Thy will be done in earth as it is in heaven.
A new heaven and a new earth.

> EARTH, that is so fair to sight
> In my sweet love's red and white,
> Hath as fair a heaven within
> Which our Lord Love sitteth in.
> O how newly, at her birth,
> He created heaven and earth!
>
> In a heaven of heavens, behind
> Her clear soul and her true mind,
> All his will is brought to be
> Perfect everlastingly.
> As within that heavenly worth,
> Lord, thy will be done in earth!
>
> In his earth thy will be done,
> In this home of night and sun,
> Blood on journey, peopled mouth,
> Fragrance of her comely south,
> Her hot east, and angry north
> Whence a cold wind bloweth forth!
>
> From thy mid perfection grow,
> Lord Love, if thy will be so,
> Till within her body's cells
> Palpably thy presence dwells,
> And her lovers, mazed and dumb,
> See in earth thy kingdom come!

Commentaries—II

Whence is this, that the mother of my Lord should come to me?

In the hill country,
    Where the streets clomb
By church and market,
    There was my home.

There from wise teachers
    Patience I learned,—
Waiting till truth be
    Rightly discerned.

Still to that teaching
    Weary I clave:—
Shall not Messias
    Mightily save?

Lo, at that moment
    Love's maid was known,
In the hill country,
    In a small town.

And to the gathered
    House of my kin
Came she, exalted,
    Suddenly in.

Commentaries—II

Then said I, 'Whence now
    Can this thing be,
That my Lord's mother
    Cometh to me?'

But in her glory,
    Near as she trod,
Sang she: 'My soul hath
    Magnified God.'

Commentaries—III

It were good for that man if he had not been born.

Happy, that man shall say who goes forlorn,
  Or exiled with Iscariot and Cain,
  Into the darkness when Love comes to reign,
Happy were I if I had not been born.

Shall I too say—when Love counts up his own,
  Banished for selfish and hid treachery
  Through all the long years that I share with thee,—
Happy were I if I had never known

That birth, that exaltation, that first sigh
  Peacefully loosed from a perplexèd heart,
  That hope for ever hungry now, that start
Of life now exiled from eternity !

Commentaries—IV

Gal. iv. 1-7: the Epistle for the Sunday after Christmas.

Duly, the Sunday after Christmas, we
Heard the epistle read, and suddenly
A great voice cried within my heart: Behold,
This is the doctrine ye have proved of old,
And in your bodies bear the signs thereof;
This is the knowledge of the sons of love.

Hear yet again: the elements of earth
Ruled in you, yea, the heir himself had birth
Among them—as the wise apostle saith;
For time and space and changing things and death
Were over you, ye dwelled beneath their law,
Nor any hope in any love ye saw
To bring you help, and all delight was dumb.

But when the fullness of the time was come
God sent his son forth, of a woman made,
Made underneath the law which ye obeyed,
Made under time and death and all that seemed
Your doom for ever, and ye were redeemed
Out of their might, out of their rule; at once
Love kindled, and ye knew yourselves for sons.

Children ye knew yourselves; enough discerned
Under those governors, from whom ye learned

Commentaries—IV

Obedience, patience, equanimity;
Now was your birthday come and ye set free
To meet your father Love, your brother Joy;
Kinship that naught shall in the end destroy,
For time and death are servants at your nod,
And ye are heirs,—and heirs of whom but God?

The epistle ended, and the hymn began
Praising Immanuel, the child of man.

Commentaries—V

' Sweet Jesus, be to me not a Judge, but a Saviour.'

FAIR Lord Love, whom in thy maid
I have baffled and betrayed,
  Sweet Love, unto me
No judge but a saviour be.

By the speaking of thy word
In the house of that Adored,
  Sweet Love, unto me
No judge but a saviour be.

By the fatal troth I swore
That shall probe me evermore,
  Sweet Love, unto me
No judge but a saviour be.

By the dark pains when I feel
What deep cuts my soul must heal,
  Sweet Love, unto me
No judge but a saviour be.

By the cooling hours of joy
Lest that suffering destroy,
  Sweet Love, unto me
No judge but a saviour be.

Commentaries—V

When old Paynim habits come,
Mastering my Christendom,
  Sweet Love, unto me
No judge but a saviour be.

When I seem, to her and thee,
Utter infidelity,
  Sweet Love, unto me
No judge but a saviour be.

In her malice or her pride
If she turn herself aside,
  Sweet Love, unto me
No judge but a saviour be.

In her sorrow or her need
If I leave her heart to bleed,
  Sweet Love, unto me
No judge but a saviour be.

Through the days that dawn and die
In a dear monotony,
  Sweet Love, unto me
No judge but a saviour be.

When that hour thou knowest not
Sees the bolt of Doomsday shot,
  Sweet Love, unto me
No judge but a saviour be.

When, divorced from all, I see
In myself Eternity,
  Sweet Love, unto me
No judge but a saviour be.

(85)

Commentaries—V

Now and in all hours of death
Hear what my abasement saith :
Sweet Love, unto me
No judge but a saviour be.

Love's Adolescence

STUNG by new needs, impatient of caress,
  With restless eyes, loose arms, and empty hands,
Wroth at his foster-parents' littleness,
  Between our hearts and in our house he stands.

To what shall he be turned? what discipline
  Of labour shall instruct this young Desire,
Who, meant as gardener or builder in
  Our territory, seems thereof to tire?

Some business, Fair, of abnegation! some
  Weary, extreme, and undelightful task,
Whence with achievement panting he may come,—
  This is the life his fretful moments ask.

To ease which petulance of comfort I
  Upon this sin or that will him employ:
But what hast thou wherewith to occupy
  Love's powers, who moves in us no more a boy?...

What, wilt thou on so long a journey trust
  His ignorant head? so mighty a design
On him, unwise in exploration, thrust,—
  Whose absence from thee also shall be mine?

Think not that thou canst this young Love dismiss,
  Orphaned, to find felicity, yet keep
As heretofore such pleasure in our kiss,
  Such rest in our companionable sleep.

Love's Adolescence

With all our eagerness must he be shod,
  With all devotion clad,—for long and large
Must be his road and passion ere that God
  He find who gave him first into our charge.

Divine the hope, divine his exodus;
  And that adventure of our all, divine!
But he must wear our whole desire if thus
  Thou send'st him,—all thy purposes and mine.

Yet furnish him, if thou wilt have him go
  Where only he his true descent may learn:
Farewell, my heart assents,—if need be so,
  I will not see thy face till he return.

Outland Travel

O WHO would climb the Andes,
   The Alps or Himalay,
While here at home in any street
The kerbstone close beside his feet
   Falls far, far, far away?

Or who would sail the ocean
   Or pierce to either pole,
While distance, parting east and west,
Is measured here by hands outstretcht
   To any casual goal?

Or who would dare the tribesmen,
   The frosts or the simoom,
While here at home in any talk
Dark heresies of evil walk
   And souls may drop to doom?

O who would seek adventure
   In Tibet or Pekin,
When he at home within his heart
May on ancestral journeys start,
   And mightier quests begin?

Advent

OUR LORD the Nameless One (blessèd be he)
Saw from his threshold in eternity
Man from earth's towers climb among the gods,
Breaking their thunders, splintering their rods,
And in the lesser heaven sit in their stead.
Then to his council of young souls he said :
' Who shall be safe from man whom We have made
Seeing already he without Our aid
Forces yon thrones and heights of deity ? '—
Even on the word there came one suddenly
Crying : ' Ah, Master, men make war on thee :
Lo, the young Christ, being alone at play,
Is by audacious ambush caught away
Into the soul of man : where, lest he dwell
For ever, follows the prince Michael—hell
Having from him but now their duty learned,
And thence his weary banners scarce returned.'

Then said the Mighty One : ' Throne under throne
Vanquished with all its cherubim may groan,
And spirit be by spirit baffled : none
Shall so from matter bring again Our Son.
None but Ourself shall join in strife with man,
Our image : a new thing since time began
Proceeded to this hour's accomplishment
Within Us : sit, ye gods, and see the event.'
He said, and hid from heaven the hallowed face,
Whose name is called *ha-makom*, or the Place.

Advent

But while he spoke, the archangel, heavenly war
Bright in his person gathered up, dropped far
Through air on air, upon man's spirit stayed,
And all his vast religious earth surveyed,
Temple and oracle, fetish and lair
Of jungle powers; then, seeking the strong prayer,
The passionate fond inexorable will
Which had pierced heaven, he moved therethrough, until
Nine months through heresy and heathendom
Had he passed on, and empty thence had come :—
Dry and ascetic deserts where no sweet
Flowers of young love grew; storms of choking heat
Under whose lust such buds withered and burned;
Sea-fogs of ignorance where he discerned
Some few unfruitful isles of rocky law,
Whereon wrecked sailors hardly dwelled : he saw
Cities wherein lay prophets starved and dead
And a great crowd of instincts cried for bread,
Or where to docile pupils learnèd scribes
Taught rote and ritual; fierce nomadic tribes
For whose wide herds their fathers' lore sufficed :
But none of all these could have seized on Christ.

At last he drew, at nightfall on a day,
Near to an Asian caravanserai,
And lo, his nostrils as he neared its square
Felt the expanding and benigner air
Which blows where gods are : entering, he found
Three companies sitting upon the ground,
Each by its fire; the prince through his worn frame
Felt the mysterious effluence of the Name
And knew his search was ended, in that khan
Reposed the audacious victory of man.

Advent

Upon the left, sweet and serene of soul,
Sat in his yellow robe and with his bowl
Our Lord Gautama, wandering through earth
To teach the law and set men free from birth ;
To whom the archangel : ' Hail, friend ! is it thou
Hast wrought the deed whereat heaven marvels now ?
Of all men's sons hast thou, the least defiled,
Broken our walls and borne away the Child
To this thy earth ? hast thou with violence
Made God thy secret of experience ? '

To whom our lord the Buddha answered : ' Hail,
Brother ! what know my people of this tale ?
Or how should Sakka of the nearer crown
And Brahma of the farther be brought down ?
Or how should souls enlightened and set free
From hunger clutch or conquer deity ?
Nay, if for this through many a thousand lives
Some uninstructed soul in good hope strives,
What profit hath he when they all are spent ?
Learn, from no god descends Enlightenment.
They pass and suffer, borne upon the Wheel
Of Being ; no content mankind shall steal
From such communion ; peace dwells otherwhere.
Lo, if thy Christ would learn it, it is here.'

He ceased, and half-abashed the prince passed by
To where amid his turbaned company
Our Lord Muhammad, girt and scimitared,
Sat brooding by his fire and bending hard
His eyes upon the Book ; but when he heard
The angel's question, half in wrath he stirred,
Answering, hot in zeal : ' What art thou then,
That o'er the Maker sett'st the power of men ?

Advent

What talk'st thou of God's Son ? know'st thou that we
Are the pledged champions of that Unity,—
Moses, and Milton, and each messenger
Sent into all lands ? and no foot shall err
From service to his kingdom, who controls
The birth and dereliction of all souls,
Alone, and their salvation ; who is Fate,
Immutable yet all-compassionate ? '

So spake our lord the Prophet ; the god turned
His face and steps to where the third fire burned
Mid a hushed company, before a maid
Helmed, with bright eyes and joyous ; elders staid
About her sat, young silent squires observed
To feed the happy embers, others served
Her captain's meal of water, meat and bread,
Waited upon her women, built her bed
Of new-mown hay and spread their cloaks thereon.
Within her face illumination shone,
And when she spoke, unto the prince was known
The voice of Godhead mingling with her own.

' O tower of ivory, crystal tower of prayer
And passion, hold'st thou then that hidden stair,'
The archangel said, ' whereby, since Babel crashed
And all men's hopes of solid heaven were dashed,
Their age-long quest hath climbed ?   Wert thou made wise
By this devout invasion to surprise
The young Child, yet console him for his rape ?
How canst thou think to guard him ? his escape
Is by Omniscience plotted, set him free
Ere yet the thunderbolt shall ravage thee,
Set free the Child, and pray that thou may'st live,
If haply the Most Merciful may forgive.'

Advent

Then said the mistress of our destiny:
' Com'st thou, O head of war, at last to me?
Now is no help; yea, if all men and I
Repented us, there were no remedy.
By one sole way shall God return to God,
Now nine months opened, till which path be trod
He shall go darkly, from his heaven divorced,
By pain and hunger shamefully enforced,
Whom to redeem avails no angel's sword;
This is a thing beyond thee, O my lord;
The Word of challenge is within me made
Flesh of my flesh; by life and death essayed
Heaven shall he reach again, we with him then.
Return: with dragons lies thy war, not men.'

And her time came upon her, and she lay
World-tended: but the prince was caught away,
And heard the young souls of divine delight,
Who dawn for ever through deific night,
Sing 'Peace': and saw the cherubim abase
Before the darkness of the riven Place
Their helmed and helpless valour, sad to know,
While the victorious Earth held God below,
What pain, what death, what solitude should be
Ere he led captive his captivity.

Christmas

WORD through the world went
  On Christmas morn:
'Tidings! behold, a
  Townsman is born!'

Then in their council
  Smiled the high lords:
'Sword for world conquest
  Mid a world's swords!
Need shall our armies
  Have of each birth,
In the last battle
  Wins us the earth.'

Still stood the priesthood
  Singing the Mass:
'Yea, is our word come
  Truly to pass?
Blessèd and broken
  Crumbs that we give,
Say: say, O chalice,
  Can a creed live?'

Christmas

Then while to Shakespeare,
  Brooding alone,
In a dark pageant,
  Lear was shown,
While his just loathing
  Hung over men,
Lo, from the darkness
  Came Imogen.

Then said a free maid,
  Heart against mine :
'Take me, lord governor,
  Who am all thine.
Thou that hast blessed me
  With a new light,
Ah, is thy handmaid
  Fair in thy sight?'

Then said our Lady,
  'Clean is the hut,
Filled are the platters
  And the door shut.
Sit, O son Jesus,
  Sit thou, sweet friend :
Poor folk have supper,
  And their woes mend.'

'Now', said our Father,
  'All things are won:
Welcome, O Saviour:
  Welcome, O Son :

Christmas

More than Creation
   Lives now again :
God hath borne Godhead
   Nowise in vain ! '

Word went through Sarras
   On Easter morn :
' Tidings, behold a
   Townsman is born.'

The Fourth Dimension

I

WHEN the True Fire leapt forth and fell through space
    On the elect, what saved them there from death
But you, O tender pitiful air, O grace
    Transformed to matter, made our mortal breath?

O their salvation was in your strong wind
    Whose matter dulled God's immaterial fire,
Whose loving-kindness did his passion bind,
    Or all the world had perished in that pyre.

Thus docilely the tongues of flame sank down,
    And, quenched to visibility, he fell
Upon their foreheads, a bright flickering crown,
    Who did himself with his soft patience quell.

II

Your great original he breathed, mild air,
    Whose risen body shone on those elect,
And did with them your benediction share,
    Yet could their bolted and dark doors neglect.

And delicately into you he passed—
    Restored unto the heavens from which he came
To be a spark on either touching vast
    Of soul and matter, making them one flame.

The Fourth Dimension

O who but you received him when he ranged
    Spirit again? what cloud but such, O grace,
As rose first out of you when you were changed
    To touch and sight between the poles of space?

O heavenly comfort, blow about us! steep
    Souls in your peace as bodies in your care!
And you, fine lungs of my risen body, deep
    Breathe you of that mild, fresh, and tender air!

Birds

STARLING to swallow
  Cried, bird to bird:
'In the sky's hollow
  What is this we heard?
What is this descends
  Where our broods fly,
From the far ends
  Of the sky?'

Eagle to vulture
  Cried, boldest thought
To the sepulture
  Where virtue is brought:
'What is this we saw
  Speedily come
As the wind's flaw
  Through our home?'

Wonder outwelling,
  Each in its kind
Rose from its dwelling
  In my lower mind;
All, above this earth
  Of my delight,
Felt the true worth
  Of their flight.

Birds

All their fast winging,
   This folk of air,
All their clear singing,
   Circled by the fair
Mystery of mind,
   Stilled as they knew
That rushing Wind
   Pass therethrough.

Listening and peeping
   From my tall house,
Heard I the cheeping
   Amid orchard boughs:
Also in the cotes
   Where dwell my loves,
Heard the soft notes
   Of those doves.

From my farm kitchen,
   Stablished in space,
Where I sat rich in
   My own time and place,
Heard I all my doves
   Coo to their kin,
As to their loves
   Love flew in.

Sleep

[IN A GUEST BOOK]

SLEEP which the Omnipotent
To man's heaving heart had sent
Was the one thing here also
Which Omniscience could not know.

Jealous that his creature knew,
Delicately then he drew
Man's soul to so fine a term
It could hold his loosing firm.

Long to wait did he endure
Till, strong, terrible, and pure,
Saw he in a stable shed
The true eyes and lonely head.

Then, Creation in his heart,
Delicately to her part
He accorded : watch she kept,
And at last Omniscience slept.

In an Ecclesiastical Procession

WHITHER ascend we now with trumpets blowing,
 And banners stiff, and incense flung abroad,
And priests upon the chanting crowd bestowing
 Blessing, and all the ministers of God?

What eyes are open in this congregation
 To see, beneath the candles' holy fire,
The victim whom we bring here for oblation,
 Behind the singing children of the choir?

Before the sacrificial priest, bedizened
 With ceremonial garb of antique guise,
What offering is borne, with cord imprisoned
 And bound with scarves upon his mouth and eyes?

Up to the altar wheels the long succession
 Of figures, moving pathwise with the sun :
Dreadful our road of ritual progression,
 Who are the heirs of all that priests have done.

Be blind, ye folk! the knives of ancient slaughter
 Drip redly here beneath the carven Christ.
Lo, Agamemnon, mourning for his daughter!
 Lo, Hiel with his children sacrificed!

Lo, where the Aztecs reach the blazing altar,
 Lo, where the Druids chapleted pass by!—
Night is upon us, sing ye lest we falter,
 Knowing what blood herein we justify ;

In an Ecclesiastical Procession

What shrines, what prayers, what terrible oblations,
    What red and overflowing stream that runs
Throughout these aisles from ancient dispensations ;—
    On us that blood be and upon our sons !

Sing, Christian folk, how for your sins' remission
    Died Innocence, of all these deaths the sum,
Of the fierce dooms, the guilty lives' perdition,
    Which were his forerunners in heathendom.

The walls dissolve, the walls dissolve about us !
    Jungle and mountain monstrously arise,
Man's past is dark within us, and without us
    Sparkles from stormy and barbarian eyes.

Sing, Christian folk ! your Christian priest advances,—
    Drown with your chant the noise of wilder drums
Calling us back to whirl of heathen dances :
    Wheel we and pause we,—lo, the victim comes.

Faster and faster censers swing before us
    Upon the paths our painted fathers trod,
Louder and louder lifts our tribal chorus,—
    Sing, Christian folk, your Christian hymns to God.

Office Hymn

Lord God, the mystics gather
  To thy familiar tones,
The sons who know their father
  Assume their judgement thrones.
With terrible assessors
  Thy seat is thronged about :
We too are thy confessors,
  Lord, hear us too who doubt !

How can our mind surrender
  Which learns not, nor our heart,
To find thee fierce or tender,
  Or see thee what thou art ?
If thou thy face art hiding
  With darkness for a screen,
Or if thy hand be guiding,
  We know not nor have seen.

What worth should be in trusting ?
  We dare not rest therein,
Whose faith may be but lusting,
  Whose self-denial sin :

(105)

Office Hymn

Yet no wise dare we falter
   In one word,—hear us so!
We stand before thine altar,
   Denying that we know.

If thou shalt come in thunder,
   And with all evil men
Whelm us thine anger under,
   While we confess thee then
Confess thou, ere thou sever
   Us from thy household true,
Lord God, confess we never,
   Knowing not, swore we knew.

Chant Royal of Feet

LIE there, my shoes, while, slow and reverently,
   As unto flutes and odes of ritual,
I dip you, O my feet, dip to the knee,
   Lift you, and watch the purging waters fall
From the clean limbs, the little ripples shy
Run swiftly over the curved toes and fly
   To join the pool that washed off the heels' stain,
   And as from pouring hands the last drops drain
Or either sole does the still surface meet,
   My mouth salutes you with a holy strain :
Blessing and honour to you, O my feet !

In what close shells and cribs of privacy
   You the laced leather daily does enthrall,
And limit humbly to attend, *servi*
   Servorum, in bond-service menial
My body's officers of rank more high,
As the abounding and bewildering eye,
   The capital lungs, the expert nerves a-chain,
   Hands the tax-gatherers,—all these you deign
To wait on, and their toil at need complete,—
   Yea, and their monarch, the most lonely brain :
Blessing and honour to you, O my feet !

Chant Royal of Feet

Consider, feet, to how great lineage ye
    Are kin, the serfs of climbing Hannibal
And they who friended Nelson on his sea;
    Think to what stools and stairways temporal
Your strong and slender brethren have drawn nigh,
Caesar's to Rome, Moses' to Sinai:
    Think on the Ardours who, in flight with twain,
    Veil with twain wings their faces, and again
Their feet must hide so: think on how the sweet
    Tears upon his the Syrian felt rain.
Blessing and honour to you, O my feet!

A little sloth, a little apathy,
    Reluctantly to follow on Love's call,
This is your most offence! well may you be
    For such delay absolved, who not at all
By agile hints and provocations sly
With hot and febrile Fancy do comply,
    Find no sin palatable, get no gain
    As mind or mouth when they their hopes attain.
Pray, little brothers, but for stronger heat
    Of speed, to follow after Love amain:
Blessing and honour to you, O my feet!

So may the dryad soul protect her tree,
    Her whole white body, wonderful and tall,
And you, the bearers of that mystery!
    So may the threads and cordage wherewithal
God does the knot of a poised beauty tie
Be never slipped in you nor useless lie!
    So may the pangs and throbs of doleful pain
    Be far from you,—swoln bone or broken, blain,

Chant Royal of Feet

Rheumatic fires, and snare of house or street,—
  And sure your tread be and your road be plain!
Blessing and honour to you, O my feet!

ENVOY

  Teach, princes, for this song's praise, not in vain,
  If me the high Muse do at all constrain,
That heavenly equilibrium, that discreet
  Balance of passion whereof song is fain:
Blessing and honour to you, O my feet!

In a Motor-bus

NARROW and long the motor-bus
　Lumbers round bend on bend:
My limbs are stiff with standing up,
　Leaning against the end
For a long hour; on either side
　From the roof three lamps depend.

This is no car wherein I ride,
　These are not men I see;
Narrow and long my coffin is,
　And driven lumberingly,
As I go onward through the dark
　And Death goes on with me.

These are the churchyard images
　My misty eye beholds;
This is no raincoat but a shroud
　My chilly body folds;
Whose limbs no mortal heaviness
　But *rigor mortis* holds.

London and God are left behind,
　Far, far behind; we go
Down through the dark night and the sleet
　To a cold country woe.
And if my soul shall yet be saved
　Nor Death nor I can know. . . .

In a Motor-bus

O as my heart beats forward now,
   And hardly does suspire,
Shall I remember, when indeed
   Death does my soul require,
How once from Golder's Green we went
   Down into Hertfordshire?

In a London Office

SEVEN bodies round me spin
Live tentacles, to snare
And drag my mind therein
Out of the open air.

Before me a blank wall
Is built; I cannot flee,
I feel the thin threads crawl
Tightening over me.

Life is blown through the room
All round me, a thick smoke;
Seven spiders spin my doom,
In a living shroud I choke.

Ah if I could but find
That tunnel which (men say)
Leads from this earthly mind
Underneath sense, away

To the clear inner land
And the spiritual sea,
And the high towns that stand
Within eternity;

Where souls can breathe at ease
The fine salt-sprinkled air,
In long walks lined with trees
Or a wide market square.

In a London Office

Ah to be saved so ! But
Earth piled within me fills
That tunnel; I am shut
From the everlasting hills.

I dig at the entering-in,
Ere the lives around me press
My mind, by the cords they spin
Caught, into nothingness.

Wildly I dig ; above
The earth falls crumblingly ;
I feel the thin threads move
Tightening over me.

Three Friends

PALSY, blindness, death—these three friends I had :
Blindness shut my eyes lest I should be sad
For the world's pain or my own sin,
Lest mind should search without or soul within.

Palsy laid hand upon me lest, my will
Looking on its task, I should fulfil
In grief and toil all the works it bade :
So, trembling, nodding, helpless I stayed.

Death was my chief love, far off dwelled he,
Comfortable promise sending to me ;
'Surely I come,' said he, 'quickly to save ;
Sweet, there is no more living in the grave.'

Woe on the day when blindness passed from me,
When cruel gods touched and bade me see,
When Death my love was from me estranged !
Palsy alone is with me unchanged.

Now can I behold the things I must do.
Death now no more is the death I knew,
Who with new life waits for me at end ;
Palsy alone still is my friend.

Three Friends

If also this pass as they passed,
And I must walk a friendless man at last,
Shall I not then long in my pain
For my blind days and their hope again?

' *Thy Will be done* '

' I prayed for you.'—From a letter.

WHAT hast thou done? what hast thou sought? Alas,
    And what shall the high God who knows thy aim
And is determined to bring all to pass
    Which by his saints required is in his name,
What shall he work upon me in delight
    So to fulfil thy purpose and his own?
O no more sacrifice me, night by night,
    But leave that prayer unto my lips alone!
For there, by many infidelities,
    My slippery soul from formal plea escapes,
But thou being once set firmly on thy knees
    Bring'st God's will on me in how many shapes!
Hallo no more those hounds upon my track:
They know thy voice; halt, turn, and call them back.

Prayer

TAUGHT by old masters, I from eyes and ears
  Through narrow passages of prayer turn in,
Seeking to find that peace the world not nears,—
  Alas, to what new roar and rhythmic din :
Great machines, mighty enginery, huge blows
  Of hammers, till my body's fabric reels
With inward manufacture down long rows
  Of tall devices, purr of banded wheels ;
Fibres and clay of being here are brought
  To workshops thick with prongs and furnaced coal,
Here melted to desire, there fused to thought,
  Here torn and crushed and bubbling into soul.
    But O what rest is here ? what place withdrawn
    Where I could lie, and wait, and feel peace dawn ?

Go not, my Lord

Go not, my Lord! why wilt thou fly?
Thou canst not fear so much as I!
What frights thee? hungry giants? They
Shall, when they know thee, beg thee stay.
Or shrink'st thou from some lurching sloth,
Some leaping rage? what is it doth
Keep thee, fair Child, from coming in?
Venture thy hand upon each sin,
To find they are not foes when once
Their manes thy touch no longer shuns!

Alas, thou'rt gone: yet 'twas, 'twas thou
Who shyly looked on me but now,
In distance safe, and would not come,
For all device, to thy new home:
Too rough, too strange, this heart appears
For thee, my God, to quell thy fears!

What can I show thee, what can say
That shall at all persuade thee stay,
If thou shouldst come again? what toy
Shall serve, what dainties, princely boy?
Rather be tempted upon me
To exercise thy bravery,

Go not, my Lord

Pluck up good heart, upon these rude
Wild aboriginals intrude!
Before those young courageous eyes,
Once thou art in, all peril flies,
And thou shalt find this world to be
The land thy Mother promised thee!

Envoy

WHO shall care for these verses when a few men are dead,
In a month when the last word, whate'er it be, is said,
That lifts up amid living names my else-forgotten head?

Nay, how shall they for even so long be prosperous? Likelier
Seems it I sole shall hear them, as a man hears the whirr
In afternoon, beside his path, of the unseen grasshopper.

Printed in the United States
92841LV00001B/141/A